Anna Pugačova

The BLISS POINT *of* *Entrepreneurship*

Build Successful Businesses by Implementing These 3 Key Ingredients

PRAISE FOR ANNA'S PREVIOUS WORK

'Your whole personality radiates strength and positivism, and the message you convey is what we need to remind ourselves every day, that it is within ourselves that we must gain the faith, motivation and focus to gain the power to carry out the actions we must to reach our goals!'

CARINA JENSLID, Controller, Economy and Planning Department, Norrbotten Region

'One thing I thought a lot about was your way of telling and expressing yourself. How you could nuance, change the tone, and enchant us with what you wanted to convey. I can probably answer for everyone in the room that we could sit for hours and listen to you. A person can take facts for about 20 minutes, then you can not listen anymore. But your way of telling was impressive! You made me feel safe. By that, I mean that you felt confident and mature in what you told. You felt strong and courageous in the subject and the reality you shared with you and I feel privileged to have received your story so openly and honestly. Keep being you and doing what you do, it works great and you influence and touch more than you think! Thanks, Anna!'

SANDRA ÖKVIST, Luleå municipality

'Thank you very much for your speech. It is incredible that you are today the happy and warm person you are, given all the horrible things you have been involved in growing up. I wish more people would share your story, preferably live. You would fill the Culture Hall's large hall which can seat 1000 people. Schools with pupils also need to have access to your story. Your story is so incredibly emotional, you touch from the depths and there were many tears from my cheeks but the heart is with me all the way. There was a lot of love in the room. Fill your heart with what you need, you are an angel among us. Thank you very much, Anna, and good luck in the future.'

MARIA SÖDERBERG, CEO DARE HR Consulting AB

DEDICATION

This book is dedicated to anyone who is crazy and brave enough to build a business, create their art, and show it to the world.

Especially for those who haven't succeeded yet or for those who have forgotten why they started in the first place.

CONTENTS

FOREWORD

Every now and again, you walk into a crowded room and there is one person in the room who seems to be in the centre of that room, radiating energy and charm like a log-fire on a winter's day. On one such day, I walked into a room of more than 2,000 people and happened to stand next to that one person; the unicorn in the room. It was no accident; I'm no stranger to understanding the power of those individuals who change the world with their own special brand of magic. The event was Tony Robins' 'Date with Destiny' and our task at that moment was to choose a partner for the next five days. The rule was that the first person you looked at, who looked back at you, would be your buddy for better or worse. I'm pretty sure all eyes were on this petite little fireball because, although she was small, her smile lit up our corner of the room in the most delightful and inviting way. BUT I was the lucky one.

Over the next five days, I got to know my new friend and found out that her name was Anna. I found out that her magical joie de vivre flowed like an ocean; it was abundant enough to share with the world and it never ran out, even on 4 hours of sleep.

Meeting Anna, you could be forgiven for believing that this girl had never encountered a single problem in her entire life; someone must have paved the streets with gold for her. What I soon discovered about Anna was that her life had been far from the easy ride. We all have stories and some people re-spond to the universe through the filter of their story. Some become victims. Some simply compartmentalize events to keep them neatly out of the way of progress. Anna neither ran away from her story or indulged in it. With each new exer-cise, I witnessed the magic of her focus and it was clear that this girl had built a muscle so strong that nothing would ever divert her from her yellow brick road. I became in awe of her resilience and her fortitude. In five days of digging deep into every corner of her life, I saw a girl who could embrace her fears like nothing I have seen before. I saw a girl who could and would find a solution to any problem. I saw a girl who had no doubt that each challenge was a gift; another magical power to add to her tool belt.

I went on to learn about how Anna had grown her business. Most people wouldn't dream of starting a business without support; whether that be financial, emotional or through a partnership. Anna had none of these and for her, nothing was missing. I have met hundreds of entrepreneurs and business owners in my lifetime. I have met those with blind enthusiasm for their product, I have met those with ambition for growth and financial rewards. In Anna, I saw something different; I saw all the creativity of an entrepreneur, coupled with an au-thentic obsession to serve. This is where her true power lies. I have rarely seen a girl who is guided so definitively by the need to give her gift. It's transparent. It's magnetic. And; it's all carefully thought out in terms of marketing, sales and team. This girl…with no support…a story that would break many… and everything against her…she just seemed oblivious to the hurdles ahead. Anna's passion allows her to fly so high that mere ground obstacles cannot affect her.

It has been my pleasure to know Anna for almost three years now. On a daily basis, I watch her give herself; this purest of energies that would make her a trillionaire if she could bottle it. But it is energy with a purpose and energy with a focus, and it is backed by her acumen and ability to turn her passion into profit.

I am so proud to know Anna; through her first book to this book; she is constantly on and producing value for her audience. Many people have esteemed knowledge but when Anna shares her knowledge you learn from a passion which is so infectious that mere obstacles will disappear for you too. Each day when I see her content online, I remember that I was lucky enough to learn from her for 5 straight days. Anna reminds me that I can either go into battle with my heavy armor or my unicorn-magic. I choose the unicorn-magic any day!

CHARMAINE DE SOUZA, Queen of the Vision at *www.BusinessMobiles.com* | Official Member of the Forbes Business Council at Forbes Business Council, London

INTRODUCTION

I spent so many years trying to find *my thing, my mission* in this world. I thought it had to be something so big and powerful that it could move Mount Everest, change economics around the world, and/or solve the global climate issue.

It turned out my mission was a very simple thing. And even though it can't move mountains, it's still very powerful because there is something incredible, empowering and magical that happens when people find their thing, discover their gifts and strengths, and last but not least, make it happen.

So it took me more that 30 years to come to this simple, but powerful realisation that my mission, my work, and my gifts are all about these two simple but powerful things. But hey, it's better late than never right?

INSPIRE. I am a lifelong creator that aims to inspire other people with my art.

TEACH. I teach hundreds of simple and fun ways to actualise those creative projects, and/or reach your goals in your life or business.

Let me explain it a bit deeper.

I am not a typical artist with a brush in one hand and a painting in another. I am actually pretty bad at painting. But I have loved to create since I was a child and still today. You will see me create speaking events, workshops, fun and easy exercises, one zillion ways to support business owners, create a class, send a package, a card, a gift etc. You name it. All I have to do is to go for a walk, or hear a human need, see something happening in the world, listen to music, etc. That is my art. My art is not a competition. I trust creativity and I create what I am guided to create. I follow my own rule: *It's more important to get-it-done than get-it-perfect because the perfect never gets done.* I will create something that will inspire you and move you and give you what you want and need the most, at the given time and moment: clarity, joy, focus, strategies, tools, strength and empowerment. I create art that aims to inspire people and move their hearts. Isn't that what art is all about? No matter if it's a painting, a course, speaking engagement or a building, it's purpose is to give the viewer a feeling. And that's exactly what I am trying to do with my art and creation every single day.

My customers and followers always ask me: *How do you come up with all those ideas?* For me it's so easy. It simply happens.

I have this gift to find countless fun, creative and simple ways to pursue the project or thing I want to create. The HOW. And help people around me to do the same. There are a million ways to start, build, or grow your business. A million ways to make ideas come to life, market and sell things, and create experiences. I want us to choose the way of least resistance. The path filled with joy, fulfilment, meaning, and simplicity. And there are so many tools and strategies that can help you with that like *The Bliss Point* for example.

I was born to be a creator and inspire people with my art. And then to take my own experiences and help those who struggle to find the way to their project.

I wanted to dig deeper so I asked myself:
Why do my courses, speeches, courses, coaching, and programs leave trace in peoples' hearts and lives and make them remember?
Can anyone do that? If yes, then how and what is needed in order for that to happen?

There are plenty of people out there with their own businesses and ideas. Plenty of people who are doing what I do.
Why then, despite the energy, effort and work they put into, are some people still not where they want or need to be? Why are they not enjoying the fruits of their work or feeling like things are shifting and changing for the better? Why are they not feeling that their ideas and businesses are growing and reaching people and furthering their lives?

Is there a simple and fun formula everyone could use and follow in order to build a successful business and touch hearts without spending decades in work overload, stress, sleepless nights and worry about finances?

The short answer is: Yes, there is! And it's simpler than you think.

This book is about how YOU can find your *'Bliss Point'* and make your business, product, or service IRRESISTIBLE and make people positively crave your products and services. It's about how you can offer an experience that people never forget that they did business with you.

Let's dive into the three simple, but powerful ingredients of *Bliss Point Entrepreneurship.*

LIFE'S PATH

I grew up in Latvia, in an orphanage with 40 other kids. I was 2-3 years old then. I was born into a very large family. I was one of 11-15 children, depending on who you ask. My parents were unable to take care of any of us, and that's how we came to be separated and placed into orphanages. I met my biological mother for the first time 4 years ago at the funeral of one of my sisters in Latvia. When I finally met her, I realized even though she was never there for me, I have learned so much from her. She and my biological father became my biggest role models, but not in a positive way as you may think. They've become an example of the life I never want to have and the person I never want to become. So in order to avoid my destiny of being doomed to be an alcoholic, homeless, drug-addicted, unemployed, uneducated, poor and hungry person, I had to do everything differently than they did to create a life where I can live and thrive.

As a young child, I could never know that I would end up here in Sweden, starting my own business and fulfilling my own goals and dreams. But luckily I am here.

It all started 9 years ago when I moved to Sweden with one suitcase in my hands. I came to the country which was so vastly different from where I came from. In Latvia, my days were filled with fear, abuse, and hunger. Here in Sweden, I was safe.

No one was hurting me. But getting here was nothing you could call 'simple'.

Moving to Sweden was a huge challenge because I couldn't speak Swedish. I knew only a couple of people. I couldn't support myself financially. I was stressed, sick, sad, and alone. And far, far away from my roots, my home country, and everything I knew. No matter how hard it was to live here, it was still so much better than living in Latvia. Going back was never an option. I was here to stay and I was ready to fight for my place under the sun.

When I moved to Sweden I faced major health issues. Besides all the stress and fear I also went through a period where my physical health was breaking down. I gained over 10 kg in a couple of months and it kept going up every day. I know that because I was weighing myself every single day. I had rashes on my face and back, major pain in my joints and knees, migraines, and a sugar addiction. Why had all of this come about when I was finally living in a better country and environment? Like many other people who have tried to solve their problems by running from them, I could never run from myself. I knew quite well what the real issue was.

While living in Latvia I never knew when the next meal would come. Sometimes it was a cup of warm tea to keep myself warm and sometimes I just had to fall asleep with an empty stomach and hope for a better day tomorrow. This was an ongoing situation for 22 years of my life, aside from those few happy years in the orphanage where we got a meal four times a day. All the dishes were amazing and I still remember the smell of home made pizza or a taste of the home baked cake. It was incredibly tasty and nothing will ever be able to replace that.

In Sweden, things were very much different. I got my first job at the nearest hotel and what I saw there shocked me. Firstly I had never in my life seen so much food and I had never in my life before seen so much food being thrown away. So I went on a mission: to save as much as I could by eating as much as I could. I couldn't stop even though the guilt and shame stemming from my behaviour were eating me from within.

Food suddenly went from being a pure luxury to something very available and cheap. Unlike anything I had experienced in my whole life. I started to buy as much food as I could afford with the money I had. Going for the cheapest products gave me a lot of food. Lots of processed food like cookies, chocolate, and bread. What I was missing for my whole life was suddenly there and available and I couldn't stop myself from over-consuming all of it. I ate everything I could get my hands on because all I knew and all I could hear in my head was: Eat while you can. You never know when, and if, the next meal is coming.

A sea of cookies, butter, jams, cereals, cakes, meat, fish, and bake-off bread available to me and I did my best to make sure all it was eaten. I obviously had this unhealthy relationship with food, and I decided to eat all I could see and whenever I could.

My destructive upbringing, all the trauma, bad relationships, abandonment of my parents, and the failure of the system which was supposed to protect me, had left many, many scars on my body, soul, mind, and spirit. When I went as far as hiding food I was eating or eating myself to sleep I knew something was deeply wrong. I needed help. I was only 22 and already so broken.

One day I decided that I had to make changes in my life and that I would start with the food I eat. I wasn't ready to deal with the mental pain, but I could at least give myself proper nutrition. I refused to allow my body to fail me at such a young age.

On my way to SFI (Swedish for Immigrants), a school where you learn Swedish, I felt within my gut that I had to do something because the way I was living was not sustainable. I was only 22 and already sick, unhappy, and poor. I wanted to feel better, so I decided that I will start to eat better to heal my addiction to food, sugar, and eating for comfort and from fear. And I knew I had to do it all by myself.

I bought what I thought was healthy food. The labels said: natural, healthy, and nutritious. And I believed them. Until I went back home, and by chance, I saw the ingredients list on one of the products. The list was long and full of names I couldn't even pronounce.

I was angry and rightfully so. I was angry because I bought an idea of the product, but the product itself was something else. I was angry because I had invested my time, energy, and money. I bought the idea of healthy food, healthy eating, vibrant energy, and nutrition. Instead, what I got was something else and I felt fooled. How can a single product contain so many ingredients, food additives, and chemicals? I was angry, I felt cheated and disappointed. This was a turning point for me and my journey to become healthy.

Firstly, I KNEW I couldn't change the food industry. I was an immigrant in a foreign country. I could barely say anything in Swedish. Why would anyone be willing to listen to me? Secondly, I KNEW this was my time to do something. So, instead of taking on a fight with the whole food industry, I decided to start my own business and create my own products. Real ones.

You may wonder why I had such an obsession with food? Because I lived 22 years of my life in hunger. Having a warm meal was the best thing that could ever happen to me both as a child and an adult. Whenever I got a chance to have food, it was the biggest joy of my day and many times the only one.

Food is not only food. Food makes us talk, connect, enjoy, explore, heal, feel, experience, learn, understand generations, history, and growth. Food is not only what we eat. Food is how we live. Food is such a huge part of our lives, traditions, history, and future. And I was on a mission and longing for all of that. Food is one of the best tools on earth. I had to take action to make a change for something important.

In August 2013 I started my very first product-based business: *'Anna's Natural'*. The idea of the product was the actual products. No misleading. No fooling anyone. My mission was to only offer clean food. I produced and sold very unique food with no food additives, preservatives, or colourings. The products were free from wheat, dairy, white sugar, milk protein, and also vegan. Handmade bread, cereals, cakes, deserts, and plant based drinks.

A better version of what's offered in the store. The products were unique. The idea was unique too.

In my home country I never thought about what I ate. Firstly, because I took what I got whenever I had a chance. And what I ate were very simple products with few ingredients, and mostly produced locally. In Sweden I had to buy everything from the grocery store. And from what I saw, I was no longer surprised why myself and so many other people have health issues.

In Sweden, almost everyone is allergic to something. That means that they have to buy or bake different things for different people so that everyone can eat. Suddenly thanks to my products everyone in the family could eat the same cake.

Through *Anna's Natural,* I learned to do business. I took care of orders, manufacturing, delivering, packaging, marketing, customer service, social media, and online courses in nutrition and health. I did everything. Thanks to *Anna's Natural* I got a chance to hold courses, food workshops, sell my products to grocery stores, hotels, and individuals all over Sweden. I was able to do public speaking, and meet other business owners. It was such an amazing journey and loved every step of it.

I was very determined to work hard and do what it takes to change people's lives and succeed in my own life and business. Still, I never really succeeded.

I struggled a lot to keep my business, my energy and economy running. I basically paid people to eat my products. I took another 4 extra side jobs to be able to support myself financially and to pursue my dream. My dream of having my own life, business, and changing people's lives for the better.

While I struggled to keep my business and health running, I also went through some major changes in my life. I struggled through major breakups and I had to, again, fight those inner demons that had been following all the way from my life in Latvia.

The one good thing that came out of this was that I got my physical health back and I was in better shape than ever before. Food wasn't my enemy anymore.

But my daily life wasn't what I wanted it to be and neither was my business. Despite all of my efforts, I barely could keep my head above the water. And still, I could feel a strong presence of hope. I hoped for a better future, a better life, and a successful business that could impact and change people's lives for the better.

I wasn't going to give up. Not yet. But I never understood how I could still not be where I wanted to be, despite all of the work, effort and love I put into my business.

I kept going for almost 6 years. In the summer of 2018, I found myself at the crossroads and I knew I had to make a decision. After all these years and all of the struggle, I was exhausted. I had invested so much time, energy and resources without it feeling worthwhile.

I was tired of working in several jobs. I was tired of late nights and mornings that started at 5 am. I was tired of not being able to support myself financially. I was tired of constantly feeling the resistance from the municipality where I was living and where my business was registered. I was tired of fighting.

I went back to a list of my core values and I asked myself: Does my current business meet at least a few of them?

Some of my core values include: time, financial stability, hope, joy, variety, and meaningful work. After almost 6 years in my business, I lost the feeling of joy. Above all, I lost the feeling of hope in my business. I was investing thousands of hours, but the reward was very little and oftentimes nothing at all. I was always stuck in work and that was all that I knew. This wasn't a sustainable lifestyle and I was longing for something more.

I was longing for the feeling of freedom, making an impact, and hope for a better future for myself and humanity. So my decision to shut down *Anna's Natural* suddenly felt very clear and obvious. I stopped baking and selling my products. I

stopped doing food workshops and guided shopping tours in stores. I stopped doing public speaking engagements about food, food additives, ingredient lists, and healthy eating. I shut down everything and quit my job as a teacher, office cleaner, and every other side job that I had.
I was done with hiding behind the kitchen, baking and packing my products. I was finally ready and open to focusing on a better well-being and work-life.

I chose to invest in and own what I always knew I was best at : inspiration and teaching. I moved these two things to the front of the line of importance. I realised that I had a way better chance to inspire and help people than standing behind the kitchen and baking healthy food products. I knew deep inside of me that I could make a bigger and better change. I could reach and serve more people by doing public speaking events, educating people through my courses, workshops, coaching and my books, instead of preparing a healthy meal plan.

I made that decision in the summer 2018. By May of 2019, I published my very first book. An autobiography which was a success in Sweden and some books were sold even to Norway and Finland. I had public speaking events booked a few months ahead from organisations and business owners from all over Sweden on topics like: motivation, organisational change, working environment, restructuring, leadership, digitalisation, marketing, and communication. As well as speaking events around my debut book.

n a year my life had changed tremendously. I worked as little as I ever had, clients and new bookings kept coming to me from unexpected places, I could take a day off, and I could finally pay myself a salary. I knew for sure, this was only a beginning of my true purpose and journey.

THE SECRET SAUCE OF THE 70S

During my first 5 years in my business, I did lots of research and study around food, food additives, health, how we human beings interact, behave, think, feel, and WHY there are so many people that struggle so much with their relationship to food. I did workshops, cooking courses, and public speaking events. I taught and inspired so many people to take what they put in their bodies very seriously.

While preparing for one of my public speaking events, I came across a term: *Bliss Point* and I haven't been able to forget it since then. Furthermore, I was so inspired, that I created my own *Bliss Point* theory.

You may wonder what the *Bliss Point* is and what it has to do with this book.

Howard Moskowitz, American market researcher and psycho-physicist, discovered the *Bliss Point* in the 70s. The *Bliss Point* is the sweet spot. The exact amount of salt, sugar, and fat that makes the food product irresistible. Through experimenting and testing the amount of salt, sugar, and fat, he could find the exact amount to make it addictive. No more, and no less, but just an exact amount of fat, salt, or sugar to make you want, eat, consume, crave, and buy more and never stop this vicious circle.

Suddenly everything became crystal clear and explained exactly why it's so hard for people to stop eating and consuming certain foods even though they understand with their minds that it's not good for them. I was one of them. But now I was on the mission to change that and educate people around me.

Then something else happened. I suddenly got an idea of taking the concept of the *Bliss Point* and turning it into something more positive while applying it to my favorite subjects: entrepreneurship, leadership, mindset, growth, and business.

So I started asking myself: *What if there was a bliss point of entrepreneurship? If yes, then what ingredients would that include? What is salt, fat, and sugar in the business world?* Honestly, it wasn't that hard to figure that out. And it clearly explained why I suddenly started to succeed in my business.
I have been working as a public speaker, educator, writer, and business coach for 8 years now. Looking back, I can see which engagements, speeches, courses, and calls have left the most impression, which has led to recommendations and new job opportunities. My work has seemed to leave both sides the giver and receiver speechless, heartfelt, and touched to tears. It was the *Bliss Point of Entrepreneurship.* When I chose this path and these three ingredients in my business everything suddenly changed. And finally for the better.

FOLLOW YOUR HEART

Let's go through all the successful entrepreneurship ingredients in the order where we start with the least appreciated. Ingredient number one is HEART.

As a leader, entrepreneur and business owner, I believe that FEELING, the heart is crucial in our lives and work. It is too often misinterpreted and/or diminished by things like logic, excel tables, numbers, charts and statistics.

We are not taught to lead by heart. To trust and follow it. What I have learned from 8 years in business working with, and talking to hundreds of people, is that it's the one that makes the biggest impact and makes our lives and work meaningful.

So as simple as it sounds, it still has to be said. Whatever you do, do it from your heart and with your heart. Motivate people and inspire them to move forward, to trust, to believe, to change, and to

HEART

Passions
Fire
Empathy
Compassion
Inspire
Connect
Inner drive
Motivation
Feelings
Trust
Believe
Why
Creativity
Joy
Energy
Vibrant
Enthusiasm
Intuition

feel. In order to do that, YOU, in the first place, have to be doing something from the heart. Something you are all fired up about. Something you can't stop thinking and talking about. Something that moves you. And when you feel that within you in your experience and being, people around you get moved too. Some may probably think you are silly, childish or a bit weird. Let them do so, but do not take it personally, or let it affect you strongly.

This is crucial. Especially when it comes to teaching. And I don't mean only classroom teaching. I mean teaching and being a leader for your people, community, clients, and colleagues. Why? Because people listen better when inspired.

Or let me put it this way.

I always say, whenever you teach, don't forget to inspire. And whenever you inspire, don't forget to teach.

Leading by the heart also means being true to yourself, doing what feels good to you, and following your soul's work. You can call it instinct or a gut-feeling. It's your job to get away from all the distractions from time to time, so you can hear your own voice and understand what it is telling you.

To trust your own abilities and power and share your gifts to the world will attract more of the right people in your work and life. Inner-strength is one of the keys to every success. If you don't trust your work, no one will. And that is not a good business plan.

No matter what I do, present, teach, write, or create, the feeling and the Heart always take the driver's seat and I trust my own power. Because only when I inspire people and move people, I can teach them something. It's only then they are ready and open to receive. Simple and powerful. Because we don't feel like doing when we are told what to do. But we can move mountains from inspired actions.

Whenever I read testimonials or what people say after my courses, speaking events or coaching it always begins with the same thing: how they feel and then what they learned or what stuck with them. Always. And every time I see it, I know I have connected both with the person's heart and mind.

Follow your heart and the hearts will follow you.

'Thank you Anna for your description of the Law of Attraction (LOA) linked to gratitude. It was like it came loose in me and I finally understood on a deeper level how LOA is connected. I have read and tested lots but have felt that it was scrapped because it was only a piece of the puzzle. You made me understand in-depth and flip, I got 3 new bookings of web help packages and a mini-course in WordPress yesterday without coming out with my video ad yet.'

JENNY SANDFORS, WEB-DEVELOPER, *www.internetform.se*

'Anna shares many keys to getting ahead with your business, no matter what your focus is. Concrete and clear tools while everything is coming from the heart. She has helped me unlock several blocks that prevented me from moving forward. There will be a clear before and after I invested in Anna's support.'

MARIA MELIN WITTBERG, PROFESSIONAL NETWORKER, Certified Coach and Firefighter, *www.mariamelinwittberg.se*

DO THE WORK

The second ingredient is ACTION. Doing the actual work, step by step.

I am not going to lie, entrepreneurship can be hard and it's definitely not for everyone. It's like always working on an unknown land. I have seen too many people spending their time practicing wishful thinking and month after month, year after year, they wonder: *Why am I not there yet?*

Another thing is that too many people stay stuck and give up too early on their projects, ideas, or business.

Clarity comes from consistent actions even if it means taking action in the wrong direction. It's still beneficial.

Thinking forward won't move you forward. Action will. But not desperate and fearful ones. Mindful, consistent and heart felt actions will take you where you want to be. It's that simple

but yet we make it so hard which is why so many of us struggle on a daily basis.

I worked and worked hard for over 20 years of my life to survive as a soul and a human being. To have food for a day, to have education, and to do all it takes in order to give myself an honest chance. To have a better life than my sisters, brothers, biological parents, my relatives and generations before me. I had felt all that trauma that went through my generation and the one before weighing on my shoulders, and it was up to me to finally break the cycle for myself and the generations ahead of me.

I chose to do the work despite the pain and struggle. And I am still committed.

I started my business back in 2013. I was 23 years old then. For almost 6 years in my business I struggled. For 7 years. Tears, late nights, early mornings, one million rejections and few moments of pure joy over the smallest victories. There was never enough despite all the work, time, energy, effort, and resources I put down. What I didn't know back then was that more doesn't always bring more. More fear-based actions won't bring you peace. More work doesn't always bring more or better results. Doing more of what doesn't work won't make it suddenly work.

Actions don't always require you to move mountains, struggle and suffer. In my case, I didn't know better back then. All I knew was suffering, over-working, over-worrying, and prioritising the small stuff, putting everyone else ahead of me and forgetting about myself. What I learned was that one small action can be as powerful as making a decision or letting go of something that no longer serves you, your business, or your life. Actions move you forward, create a positive feeling, and provide momentum and clarity in your business and what your next step should be. Everything starts with a single thought, but it's action that brings those thoughts and ideas into life.

I am here today because I made so many right AND wrong decisions and steps and I chose to keep going. Doing things gives you self-confidence, experience, empathy and love for yourself and the art, business or project you create; which can't be taught in school.

Don't give up. There is no such thing as an overnight success and you know it.

'I chose Anna as my business coach to help me with strategies in my company. I did it because I want someone who really listened to what I want with my company and where I was somewhere so I could take my company towards my dreams and goals. That was the best I could do! Anna has the heart, the strategies and she saw and listened to what I needed. The fact that she then delivers both messages and concrete tools kindly and clearly meant that in just over a month I had earned the money I had invested in hiring Anna. With heart, passion and clear tools, I can now achieve exactly what I want in my company. Do you also want to do it, hire Anna, it will be the best you have invested your money in.'

NINA BERG, CEO of "Nina Berg - A Kick in the Ass". Author, Lecturer and Motivator, *www.ninaberg.se*

'Thank you so much, Anna! I am still living on the energy and planning that is black and white from your workshop and going into the weekend knowing that I will do exactly what I am going to! Thank you!'

IDA SUNDMARK, Educator at Apan Grus, *www.apangrus.se*

'I'm active on social media in a way I have never been before.
I set goals for the day and end them. I think about more and
have an intention with my doing. I have become more courageous and learned a lot of new things at a paltry 5 days. Think
how I will feel in 11 weeks !!! Thank you for a cruel week!'

MATILDA CAVANAGH, L.I.F.E COACH - Living Intentionally
for Excellence, *www.matildacavanagh.com*

KNOW YOUR THING

I always want you to feel that you KNOW what you are talking about, that you know your thing and do it well. And at the same time we put so much value in the theoretical and academic that we forget the power of experience.

Don't get me wrong, theoretical knowledge is very very beneficial, but I dare to say that experience and practical skills are higher in the rung.

How many of us have a secondary school degree in chemistry? I do. Basically everyone does who ever went to school. And now if I gave you an equation would you be able to solve it? Most likely no.

This is exactly what happens when we learn something theoretically, but the knowledge has no connection with our daily lives, work and daily to-dos.

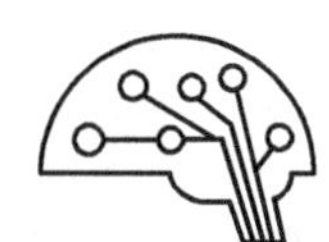

Knowledge is like a flower. As long as you pay attention to it, water it, and give it attention and sun, it will bloom and grow. The same metaphor applies to what you know. Knowledge isn't power by itself. Knowledge is power only if you use it. It's not enough only with knowing.

Having such a huge life-experience and adding all the years from my business to it when I struggled and failed so many times, I have gained a decent level of both theoretical and practical knowledge and experience which is serving me greatly in my business today.

What I also want to add here is the knowledge of the right tools, strategies and systems you need in place in order to pursue your thing: your idea, business, dream, or goal. It's about knowing the HOW. When you combine your heart and passion with the right tools, magical things start to happen. At the same time, it's hard for me to tell you to follow this ONE tool today and your business will peak tomorrow. Different branches require different tools, strategies, systems, and experiences. Your job is to end everything that is not suiting what's best for you at the given time and place in your business and work. How? By experimenting, implementing and giving things time and an honest chance to succeed. Because what I see too often is people trying out one tool and then after a week they give up and try to move onto something else. Good things usually take more than a week. What you actually need is patience. Patience is a tool, too.

'Your lecture gave effect to one of the finance and planning managers in a healthcare division, he posted a picture yesterday based on your lecture and your strategies, which are about our organization and how we can change healthcare and its working methods.'

CARINA JENSLID, CONTROLLER, Economy and Planning Department, Norrbotten Region

'I loved your workshop. Such nice inspiration and concrete tools. In-depth and outside ourselves. Magically!'

JENNY SANDFORS, WEB-DEVELOPER, www.internetform.se

'My thoughts and reflections after seeing this amazing workshop from start to finish: I felt it opened my heart to my hidden fears that I would otherwise not want to highlight. Energising and wonderful to bring new thoughts into consciousness. I am an amazing person just as I am. Smile, be happy, and believe in me, so will others do. My expertise is needed.'

MARIA MELLIN, HEALTH AND LIFESTYLE THERAPIST

'Thank you very much for yesterday, Anna! I have sent your email to everyone at work. What a huge difference it was to come to work today, of course in a positive way. I fell asleep with a smile in my soul. I was a bit nervous yesterday about how everyone would take this, but it went really well.'

KATARINA NORMAN, STORE MANAGER at Ahlsell, Gällivare

YOU FAIL WHEN

In short, all you need to understand and experience the *Bliss Point of Entrepreneurship* are these three simple, key ingredients:

1. *Knowledge* on the subject/thing you are doing today and/ or want to do in the future. I am not only talking about theoretical knowledge. Practical experience is equal if not even more valuable. Also the knowledge of the tools and strategies available to you.

2. Action. It's very simple. You have to take action towards your desired outcome. Period. Do not underestimate the power of small actions. Rome wasn't built in one day, but it was definitely built every day for a very long time.

3. And last, but not least, *have a heart and passion for what you do and want.* Keep that fire alive. Let the light, the heart guide you and your daily actions and choices. Trust it.

But here is the problem which I have seen in my work with business owners, startups, entrepreneurs, corporations, and organisations. It is a misbalance between those 3: heart, action, and knowledge.

The misbalance can show its face in numerous ways and combinations and you will do best for yourself to understand your situation, but here are few examples.

High in heart/passion and low in action and knowledge.

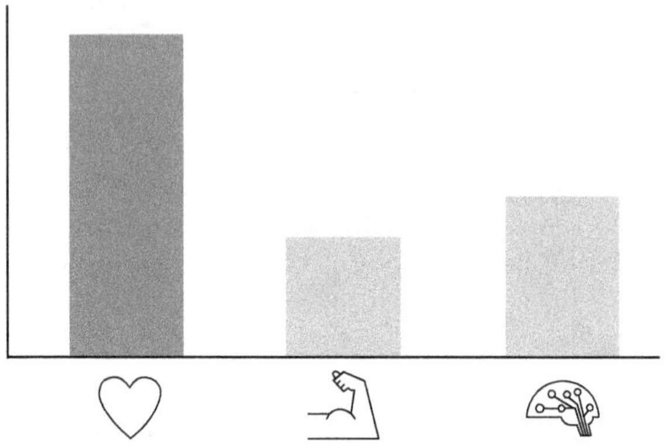

People who are new in their businesses, ideas, or organisations are very enthusiastic and all fired up about the thing. They can do and will do anything anytime to get the message/product/idea out there.

At the same time, this person may lack, for example, theoretical knowledge, the right tools, strategies, and/or practical experience. Which are an essential part of a successful business.

So this means, you are still learning. Also, the feeling of frustration and stagnation can appear because, despite all the energy, passion, and willingness to do the work, the results may still not be there.

Who are they? It's often young people. Someone who is new to something and/or someone who starts a new and exciting journey.

Let's change some things around in the same chart.

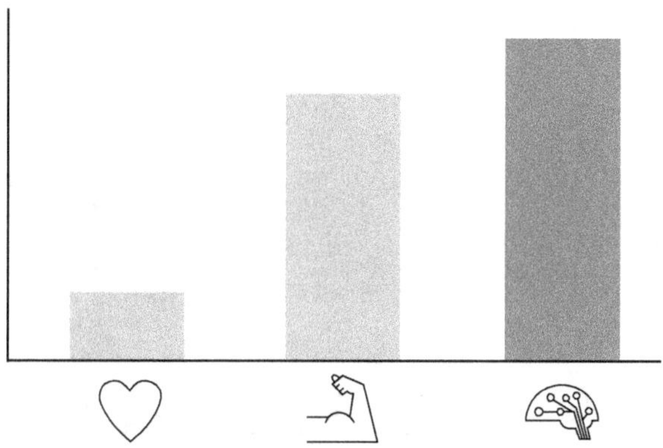

So, as you see the knowledge is high up now. This may be a person who has lots of experience, knowledge, and many, many years of work on their resume. Everything between 10-50 years. This may sound like a perfect scenario but…

What I have seen too many times is that this person may brag about all the years in business, success, and knowledge but he or she has lost their heart and passion in that very thing that got them where they are today. Or they take things for granted and say: I KNOW.

This person teaches from the mind, but seldom reaches the heart of the listener. They will tell you what to do, what's the right thing to do and/or will show you how to do it. But because of the way the knowledge is delivered, the listener will not feel inspired to action.

Who are they? It's often more experienced and older people, professors, someone who has done their thing for 30+ years; people who ask for lots of respect because of their status.

Older organizations and cooperatives with the mindset: This is how we have always done it and this is how it should be done. People who struggle with change and new things.

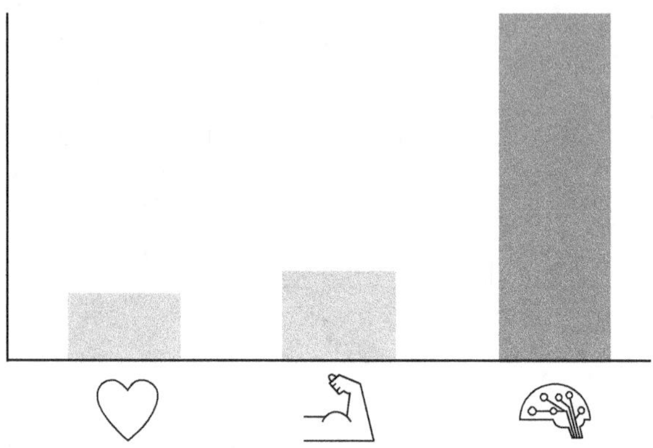

The third and last example is: high in knowledge, low in actions and heart. This is a very common combination among the scared people, who struggle with trust, and/or are experiencing Impostor syndrome.

Sometimes we get paralyzed by our knowledge. Fear of failure stops us from taking action. And low self-esteem, insecurity, or lack of trust make us feel unworthy of success.

The person may know exactly what to do, but is scared to do so. Especially if the person tried already once and it didn't work. The fear of failure and Impostor syndrome creeps into the heart and soul and sabotages your path to success.

Who is this? I am sorry to say this but it's mostly female entrepreneurs and business owners with brilliant ideas, dreams, and goals, but with low self-esteem and the fear of being caught or feeling like a fraud. I wish that more women learned from the early age their value and gifts they have been gifted with. The world needs them every day.

So as you can see, combinations can be many and different, as are the reasons. Also, I should mention that the combinations and levels of heart, knowledge, and action may vary as time goes by and you change, your ideas change, and the world around you is changing too.

Can you guess your combination? How would it look? Paint it for me, please. Thank you!

  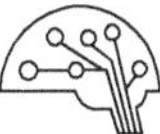

THE BLISS POINT OF ENTREPRENEURSHIP

So the *Bliss Point of Entrepreneurship* lies in finding the fine balance between a certain amount of heart, knowledge and actions. Not too much and not too little, but the exact amount of all of those three ingredients. The balance between what you feel, what you know, and what you do that is the core of your message and your business.

After reading the previous chapter, can you start to see what ingredients you are lacking? Is there anything you need to change or shift in order to experience this balance, the *Bliss Point?*

In order to experience the *Bliss Point of Entrepreneurship* these 3 elements: HEART, KNOWLEDGE and ACTION have to be in balance. They have to work together.

The problem often lies in for example:
- Some people know a lot, but do nothing about it. Knowledge is power...only If you use it!
- Some people do and act without actually thinking or having a clear intention behind their actions. Doing more of the wrong thing won't make it right.

Some people have the motivation and will, but they lack experience and knowledge.

The most important thing for you is to find YOUR Bliss Point of Entrepreneurship.

And the *bliss point* for you won't be the same as the *Bliss Point* for someone else. Some of you probably need more of knowledge, or experience or some of you probably need more of WHY, motivation, or take more action.

**So the question is:
what's YOUR Bliss Point of Entrepreneurship?**

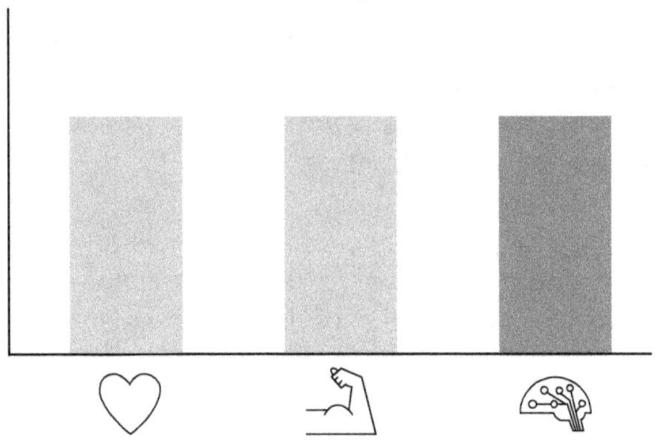

If you need help you can ask yourself

HEART: Why am I doing this? What's my driving force? How can I be even more of service? What do I need the most right now?

ACTION: Is there anything I have to do? What's my next step? How can I stay consistent in my action?

KNOWLEDGE: Is there anything I can learn? Is there anything I need more understanding about? Do I need to ask someone? Maybe do research? Gain more experience? Read?

Here are some examples of actions you can take in order to balance out **ACTION** if thats what you need:
- Write down your idea, your dream, or your goal.
- Turn off your phone.
- Set timers.
- Make a call.
- Get accountability.
- Tell someone about your plans.
- Work on your mental blocks.
- Whatever it is, get-it-done instead of trying to get-it-perfect because the perfect never gets done.
- Make mindful decisions every single day.
- Start to say yes to things.
- Start to say no to things.
- Give yourself permission.
- Make a call.
- Declutter what's old in physical space and mind space.
- Make a plan.
- Look at the numbers.
- Hire someone.
- Ask for help.
- Upgrade something in your life.

Examples of actions you can take in order to balance out HEART if that's what you need:
- Have a play time.
- Believe in yourself and your ideas.
- Do daily or weekly check-in's with yourself.
- Practice heart opening guided meditations.
- Write or journal.
- Fill your environment with beautiful things.
- Choose your path.
- Explore your creativity.

- Tell and share stories.

Remember WHY you are doing this and why you started this in the first place.
- Go through your old dreams, goals and notebooks.
- Be in nature.
- Pick flowers.
- Read a book.
- Make love.
- Go to a hairdresser.
- Make a list of your 10 favourite jokes and share them.
- Start a collection of any kind.
- Do anything thank makes you laugh, forget all that needs to be done and feel fulfilled and connected.

Examples of actions you can take in order to balance out **KNOWLEDGE** if that's what you need:
- Reach out to people who already do, know and are who you want to be, know and do.
- Ask questions.
- Practice your knowledge every single day.
- Offer partnerships and collaborations.
- Let people try your offers and/or products.
- Slowly start to work on and shift from consuming the knowledge to creating your own.
- Read.
- Keep your eyes and ears open.
- Learn about different strategies, tools and systems.

What I also have learned in my last 2 years in my business of educating and inspiring people, is the power of simplicity. Simple ideas get things done. Creativity is also a big part of my teachings. So here is a simple and creative idea for you to find YOUR unique *Bliss Point* in order to be able to give a *Bliss Point* experience to yourself and your people.

Heart: This is non-negotiable and I hope you know that yourself too. Whatever you are doing, I hope you are doing that from and with your heart. It doesn't have to be a miracle, but it has to be something you are all fired up about and believe in strongly.

Problem: There must be some kind of void in the world, a problem which you must be willing to fill or solve. If you listen carefully to your people you will know exactly what that problem is.

Solution: From all of your knowledge and experience create a product (you probably already have that) that is going to fill that void and solve the problem.

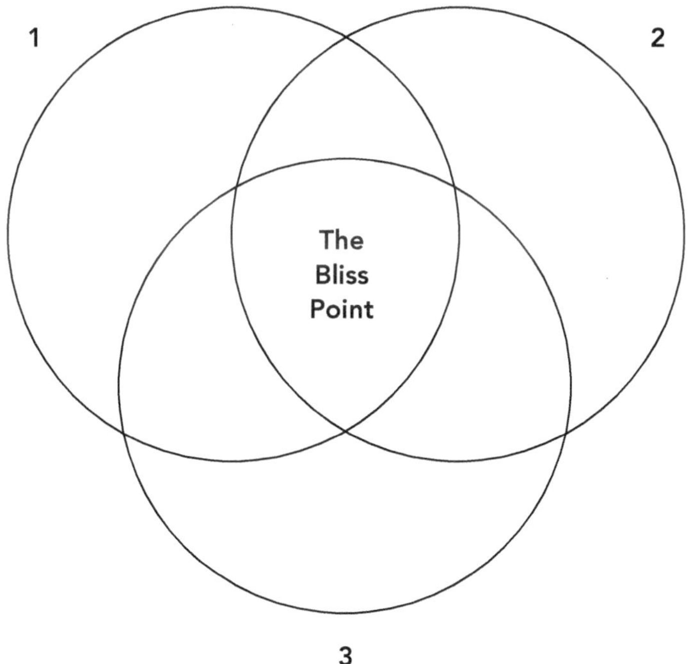

The thing I am passionate about is:

____

____

____

____

The problem I have solved or can help to solve is:

____

____

____

____

The product I can offer in order to solve the problem and fill the void which is in alignment with what I enjoy, love and are post passionate about is:

____

____

____

____

I told you, easy right? And creative.

And here is another one.

Journaling prompts. 15 questions to help you to discover YOUR *bliss point.*

1. What is the one thing that keeps coming up in all of your conversations?
2. What is the last thing you think about before you fall asleep?
3. What is the one thing (or two) you have heard someone saying to you that you can't do it or that it's impossible?
4. What is the one thing you get both passionate and stubborn about?
5. Who needs to hear your idea today?
6. What if there was enough time?
7. What if there was more than enough money?
8. What if there was more than enough love?
9. What if you had more than enough energy?
10. Who do you dream to be as a child?
11. What are all the reasons you will succeed?
12. If you knew exactly what to do...what would you do?
13. How will your work benefit you?
14. How will your work benefit your loved ones?
15. Who needs you the most right now?

THE BLISS POINT EXPERIENCE –
MAKE THEM CRAVE YOUR PRODUCTS
AND SERVICES

I always wonder what makes a unique business unique? What makes unforgettable experiences unforgettable? What makes successful businesses successful?

Have you ever experienced the following?

You read something, hear something, get something that looks almost perfect. Everything is there but still something is missing….

A feeling?

And you jump off, you say no, or you simply change your mind.

Or you read something, see and hear something, or you get something that's a bit messy, slightly chaotic, imperfect, different, almost a bit weird but despite all of that….

It FEELS GOOD!

And you give it a try, you feel excited, you say yes and give it a high 5.

Oftentimes, it can be basically the same thing you are being offered. A product, service or an experience, but the difference is not in the details or techniques. The difference lies in the FEELING of the a product, service, or an experience and opportunity.

The reason is as simple as it can be. That's because we are humans. We love and crave connection in all areas of our lives. We want to feel moved and touched by something. Something that gives us a feeling in a stomach, butterflies, awakens our imagination, or love and inspiration. Something that makes us j

So here is the big truth. Times are changing. And it's happening fast. People are searching for different things today then lets say they were 20 years ago.

People seem to be searching for more meaning, new experiences and unforgettable moments to cherish for the future. Everyone seems to be looking for a treat.

This means that we as business owners and entrepreneurs are up for a challenge.

And here is why.

The world and the business is not what we have been taught it is. The time when a standard business plan was enough to start, build, and develop a successful business is over. It's gone.

How can we as entrepreneurs and business owners give a *Bliss Point* experience to our people? How can we make them crave us in a positive way?

Because from where I stood It didn't seem to be enough with

passion for something and willingness to do the work no matter how hard it is. And then here it was...the *Bliss Point* which explained so many things in my own business and in my work with others.

The answer is simpler than you think.

In order for people to crave your products and services like people crave sweets and sugar you will have to offer something deeper than simply a solution to a problem. Something like:
- Unique personality.
- Personal care.
- Ability to listen behind the words and what is actually being said.
- Something different than anyone else in your branch.
- More meaning.
- Thoughtfulness.
- Great service.
- Sometimes going the extra mile.
- Offering quality.

And of course your skill set and your work.

Also, consider offering not only what people want/order, but what people actually need. There is a huge difference between those two ideas. As an expert in your field and business, you need to know what that is.

What I see in my courses, coaching, and speaking events over and over again, is that people come there because they want something. And this is what we all do. We go where we can get something. But if we got only what we wanted we wouldn't be satisfied. When I prepare for my work I always do the thing I am booked for. I basically deliver the product. But what makes people remember our meetings, conversations, my courses and speeches is this: I gave them something they needed, but they weren't aware of that. People may want to have success, change the world, and be millionaires, but what this is actually about is people wanting to be seen, appreciated, and heard. The feeling that I can decide over my time, that I can support myself and my family, or as simply is the feeling of that I am doing meaningful work or that I am a meaningful piece of this world. That's all. All it is, is a feeling. If you can give that to your people, that is, the feeling, and in addition to that give them what they want (solutions, strategies, etc.) they will have the *Bliss Point* experience and they will crave your products and services over and over again.

SUMMARY OF THE BLISS POINT

Time gives a perspective and a better understanding of what was going on. Looking back on my first 6 years in the business I can see why I struggled in my first food and product-based business *Anna's Natural.*

My heart and passion were definitely in the right place. I was all fired up about health and healthy food, and I was so ready to give my contribution to a better and healthier world where people do not have to suffer in their bodies and health.

My actions clearly showed my passion for this topic. I was never tired and always ready and willing to do more. It somehow seemed impossible to empty my energy and resources for a very long time. I rarely asked for anyone's permission. I simply did what had to be done, no matter how big or small it was. And I was always ready to do more, to go the extra mile, and to give more.

I also had lots of knowledge and life experience from both my home country, and many, many years in educating myself about the food, food additives, how our mood and behavior is affected by what we eat, how the food industry and companies are fooling everybody, how different food products interact with each other in baking, how to make small but meaningful changes in people's lives when it comes to food and lifestyle, and last, but not least, the mindset work around self-esteem, body image, and the strength needed to make a change.

While all of the above seemed to work greatly, there were a few, but crucial things that I was missing. And if I had more experience, I could see, for example, the importance of right timing, geographical location, or experience in the food industry

- Despite doing so much of the right thing the timing was totally out of alignment. I was a pioneer, out too early, with the idea that was too far away for too many people. Today almost 8 years later the market looks different. People are way more conscious and open to what's going on in the world and the food industry and how we together, one by one, can change both our health and planet for the better by choosing better food. Also it's worth remembering that new and unknown ideas are often criticized and dismissed before they get credit. Too many people are born to be skeptical about what's different and unfamiliar. All they need is time. Some more, and some less.

- Let's talk about the second thing: geographical location. Back then I lived in a very small city in the northern part of Sweden (actually a city above the polar circle, that's how north the city was) in a mining community. If I had my business in Sweden's capital, Stockholm, the climate for my business would have been a different story. I remember back then traveling down to Stockholm, shopping for clean ingredients for my baking, but it wasn't sustainable in the long-term and the flight took five hours round-trip. Stockholm had many like-minded people, and similar businesses, and business owners which contributed to the growth of the healthy food industry.

- Last but not least, I didn't have enough experience in the food industry. Honestly, when I went in, I had no idea what a monster I was going to deal with. Ugly truths came forward, one after another and I could see who were the bosses in this branch. The environment and food office in the municipality made decisions in favour of big food companies. Municipality where I lived back then and the whole system was against my idea and my business, despite my desperate work and attempt to help people to improve their lives and health. And I was about to lose this game.

So in short, my *Bliss Point* had plenty of heart and actions, but despite all the knowledge around and about the food and health, I was missing experience big time. Admittedly, that is why I never reached the *Bliss Point* in my first business.

The work I am doing today has a different story. Becoming a writer and stepping into my God-given gift to be a public speaker to inspire people, and becoming a business coach and educator, has open so many doors for me and changed lives for the better for so many people.

What is my *Bliss Point* today? Some things haven't changed and some things I have finally embraced.

I work from the heart, always and people feel and notice that.

I take actions every single day to keep moving forwards, helping people, and having meaningful work and life. Often, it means doing less and not working harder, rather doing more of what works over and over again.

Throughout all these years of hard upbringing, hard work, fighting, trying, getting up over and over again, and never giving up I have gained so much theoretical and practical knowledge and experience that is serving me greatly every day of my work.

Today, being a 31 year old (young) woman and having my own business for 8 years, I do a quarter of the work that I did in my first years. I feel deep in my bones that my work is meaningful and I am changing people's lives for the better. I can finally support myself financially and I am taking an official vacation for the first time in my life.

That's a true *Bliss Point* life.

FINAL THOUGHTS

There is no magical recipe for Your *Bliss Point*. I can't tell you if you need 5 extra pounds of heart or 2 more inches of experience for your *Bliss Point* to be properly balanced. It's unique for everyone and it's always changing and shifting. You have to experiment and check in with yourself once a week, or once a month to see where you are, what needs to be adjusted, or if there is anything else you need to add or remove, do more or do less of, etc. (Remember, it's not always about doing, having, and adding more.)

Let your heart take a drivers' seat and fasten your seatbelt. You are going to experience a shift.

Never stop learning things in your industry and stay up to date. Practical experience often turns out to be more valuable than theoretical knowledge.

Action will bring your clarity. Do something every day for your long term goal and do less of the fast-rewarding activities like for example: social media, answering an email, etc. Do more things that will reward you in the future, even if you can't see the immediate result right away.

Expect a miracle. Things can change for the better very fast if you choose to be open to that.

Sometimes all we need to do is to make a single decision that can change everything.

Small things can make a big difference. Plant seeds wherever you go but do remember to nurture those seeds too.

Keep creating your art. That is your main work every single day. Every project/thing you create has its journey and soul. You never know where that can lead you.

Focus down, and narrow down for a better focus. Feeling overwhelmed often comes from doing too much at the same time.

Ask for help if you need it. I am here to help and support you. One aha-experience, a single word or thought can create great change and clarity.

Be brave enough to trust your heart more. As long as you are being true to yourself and following your instincts, the rest is learnable and doable. Because, isn't life's highest purpose to be true to yourself? Stay true to yourself in your work and life.

Find out more about The *Bliss Point*, speaking engagements and workshops at:
www.annapugacova.com/bliss
Email: info@annapugacova.com
Instagram: @anna_pugacova
Sign up for Anna's newsletter at: *www.annapugacova.com*

ABOUT THE AUTHOR

Anna Pugacova, 31, is a public speaker, writer, business coach, and educator and lives in the northern part of Sweden, Luleå. She is working with other business owners, solo-entrepreneurs, cooperatives, and individuals to help them to pursue their life and work goals. She also has an online school with multiple courses and programs where she teaches about leadership, personal development, self-love, and the power of doing what you love, trusting your heart, and learning while we are alive.

Her work is known in Latvia, Scandinavian countries, and internationally as she has inspired thousands of hearts through her travels, speaking engagements, and work with other leaders and business owners.

28 August, 2020, she is celebrating her 8th year in business. As you may know (if not, now you know) '8' is her favorite number for several reasons.

She was born in 1988, 8th of December

Her identity number in an orphanage where she was placed only a couple of years after her birth with another 40 children, was 8. It means that all her clothing, sheets, etc. were marked with number 8.

She emigrated to Sweden at age 22. During her 8th year in Sweden, she published her first book, an autobiography 'Mig krossar du aldrig' - min resa från att överleva till att leva. (translation: 'You Will Never Break Me: My Journey From Surviving to Living'). In the book, she speaks about her difficult childhood with mental and physical abuse, poverty, hunger, and a dream of a better life. Despite all the struggle and pain, she inspires people to turn their fears into a driving force and never stop fighting for your dreams. Thanks to her book and all the publicity, Anna and her story have been featured and multiple newspapers all over Sweden.

And now celebrating her 8th year in business, she can finally breathe out and say: 'Yes, I did it! I finally succeeded!' This is not one of those overnight success stories. With this book, she is celebrating and honoring all of those years of hard work, resilience, decisiveness, sweat, and tears.

Anna is a motivational speaker, entrepreneur, and full of creative and simple ideas on how to make our lives, businesses, and the world a better place. In her work, she inspires and motivates people to find their driving force to fulfill their dreams in work and life because as we both know everything in life is connected.

Today she is doing both: traveling around Sweden with her motivational speeches and workshops and offering her services, programs, courses, and coaching in the digital world.

For more information about Anna's work, services and upcoming events go to *www.annapugacova.com/bliss*
Email: info@annapugacova.com
Instagram: @anna_pugacova
Sign up for Anna's newsletter at: *www.annapugacova.com*

GRATITUDE

I am so grateful for every human being who believed in my products and services from the very first day I decided to start a business. Thank you, wherever you are today for buying my healthy food products, booking coaching calls, workshops, courses, public speaking events and my book. Without all of you I wouldn't have a business today!

Thanks to all my dear friends, fans and cheerleaders in the online world all over the world and IRL for your love, support, comments, shares and recommendations.

Mattias Leijon - thank you for your love and support throughout this project. Thank you for believing in my ideas.

My accountability partner and dear friend Laura Diane Soer. Having you on this journey with me, sharing life and business journey with you has been invaluable. Keep sharing your gifts to the world.

Charlotte Lindmark – I am so grateful we met and can share both success, failures, tears and laugh with each other.

Charmaine de Souza thank you for showing to me what's possible. You are a role model for me for what a successful woman looks and feels like. I am deeply grateful to this day that you chose me as your partner for the next five days at the Tony Robbins Date With Destiny event. (And thank God I chose you!)

Thank you Facebook, Luleå for contributing almost three-thousand dollars to this project. Its a huge support for a small business owner like me. Thank you!

And last but not least – Tiny Book Project team – without you guys I wouldn't hold this book in my hands. Lindsey, Alexandra, Andrew and Lucy – you are the real heroes.

Author/Publishing Company: Anna Pugacova AB
Contact Information: annapugacova.com,
info@annapugacova.com

Ordering Information:
Quantity sales. Special discounts are available on quantity purchases by corporations, associations, and others. For details, contact Anna Pugacova AB, info@annapugacova.com or goo to www.annapugacova.com

The Bliss Point of Entrepreneurship/Anna Pugacova
1st ed.   ISBN 9789151965017